Jesus' First Miracle

Randal Gilmore

Illustrated by Dori Durbin

EXALT Publications
Fishers, IN

ISBN: 978-1-7325000-9-9

Long ago, when Jesus lived on the earth,
he did many wonderful things to help people.

Jesus healed the sick.

He fed the hungry.

He made blind people see.

He made deaf people hear.

He even made . . .

dead people . . .

live again.

We call these good deeds miracles.
Jesus' miracles are special because they show the power

God gave to him.

If God gave you the power to do miracles,
what would you do first?
Would you heal the sick?
Feed the hungry?
Cause the blind to see?
The deaf to hear?

Here is the story of Jesus' first miracle,
and the story of why Jesus kept it a secret at first.

One day, Jesus and his disciples were invited to a wedding.
Jesus' mother, Mary, was invited too.

The new bridegroom thanked everyone for coming . . .

and served a delicious meal for his guests to enjoy.

But soon there was a problem.

The servants ran out of wine for everyone to drink.

When Mary found out she told Jesus, "They have no wine."
Mary hoped that Jesus would do something to help.
She wanted everyone to notice him and his power.

But Jesus told Mary, "My hour has not yet come."
Jesus meant that it wasn't the right time for
everyone to notice him.

The right time would come later, when Jesus would be lifted up in front of everyone to die on the cross.

For now, Jesus wanted to show his disciples why they should believe in him, and not just follow him around.

Mary turned to the servants and said,
"Do whatever Jesus tells you."

Jesus told the servants, "Fill up six large stone jars with water."
Then Jesus said, "Pour some out and take it to the master of
the wedding meal."

Jesus knew that he had turned
the water into wine.
It was his FIRST miracle.

Is that what you would do FIRST . . .

If God gave you the power to do miracles?

The master of the wedding meal tasted the wine that the servant poured for him.

Then the master of the wedding meal said to the bridegroom, "Congratulations for saving such a good wine until the end of the meal!"

But the servants knew the secret of what really happened.
So did Mary and Jesus' disciples.

Jesus knew that Mary and the disciples would remember words from the
Prophet Isaiah many years before— that someday a Savior would come
to the earth and make everything new.

Isaiah said that when the Savior comes, he will invite people to a delicious meal, like a wedding meal, only with food and drink for everyone.
Isaiah said: "On this mountain the Lord of hosts will make for all people a meal of rich food, a meal of well-aged wine, of rich food full of marrow of aged wine well-refined."

"It will be said on that day, 'Behold, this is our God; we have waited for him, that he might save us. This is the Lord, we have waited for him; Let us be glad and rejoice in his salvation.'"

That is why Jesus made turning water into wine his FIRST miracle.

He wanted to show Mary and the disciples that he is the savior Isaiah wrote about— the One with the power to make everything new.

On that very day, Jesus' disciples stopped just following him around. They started instead to believe in Jesus as the Savior God promised.

But, what about the servants?

Why did Jesus let the servants know the secret of what really happened?

Because Jesus wanted the servants and everyone else who hears this story to know— the invitation to the Savior's meal is for everyone who believes, including lowly servants . . .

. . . and ordinary people like you and me.

Announcing...

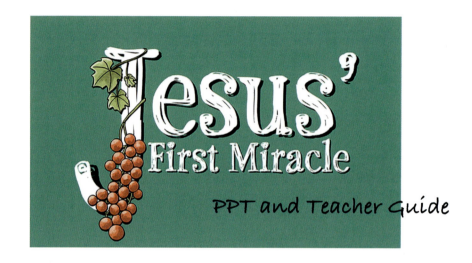

A Resource for Teachers
Available on **ExaltPublications.com**

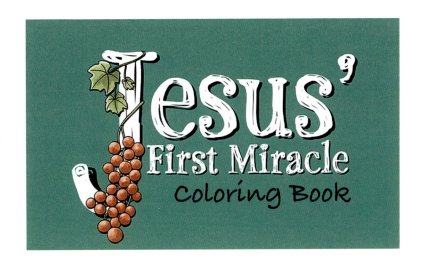

Jesus told the servants, "Fill up six large stone jars with water."
Then Jesus said, "Pour some out and take it to the master of
the wedding meal."

Available on **ExaltPublications.com** *and other sites*

About Randal Gilmore

Randal Gilmore (Doctor of Religious Studies, Trinity Seminary, Newburgh, IN) is the Founder and Director of The Gospel Story-arc Project, a ministry initiative that uses the science of story to aid in Bible exposition and better tell who Jesus is. Randal is the author of numerous books, including **The Sparrow and the Tortoise, Exalted Lord**, and **Story Deep**.

Randal lives in Indiana with his wife, Dale. Both enjoy serving the Lord and spending time with grandkids.

About Dori Durbin

Dori Durbin is a Christian wife, mom, Children's book author, illustrator, podcaster, and book coach who after experiencing a life-changing illness followed her passion for creativity and fitness, quit formal teaching, and began reaching families through writing kids' books. Dori wrote her "Little Cat Feelings Series" for kids and parents to emotionally connect earlier in life. She also coaches experts and aspiring authors on how redesign their message into purposeful and fun kids' books.

Other Books by Randal Gilmore

The Sparrow and the Tortoise

A thirsty sparrow searching for water to drink discovers the Mirror Pond at the base of Mt. Fuji. Will the pond's crystal clear water satisfy the sparrow's thirst? Or will something else become an even greater concern? Entertaining for all ages.

Exalted Lord: A Study of Jesus Christ's Exaltation From the Book of Acts

Discover why the Apostle Paul gave up everything for the sake of knowing the "Exalted Lord." Unravel stories of persecution, testing the Lord, and the dangers of succumbing to Satan's control. Then go further than ever before in your own love for Jesus as you grasp the profound significance of his exaltation as Lord.

Story Deep: How to Find Hidden Treasures of Meaning as You Study Bible Stories

Learn how to go beyond Roman numeral outlines and word studies to explore the rich depositories of meaning found in biblical narrative. A detailed guide for your own expository study of Bible stories.

Available on **ExaltPublications.com** *and other sites*

Made in the USA
Monee, IL
19 December 2024

74667116R00024